Fourth Grade Advanced Math Book

Multiplication and Division

Speedy Publishing LLC
40 E. Main St. #1156
Newark, DE 19711
www.speedypublishing.com

Multiply in Columns

Solve.

1. $\begin{array}{r} 97 \\ \times\ 7 \\ \hline \end{array}$

2. $\begin{array}{r} 11 \\ \times\ 4 \\ \hline \end{array}$

3. $\begin{array}{r} 21 \\ \times\ 8 \\ \hline \end{array}$

4. $\begin{array}{r} 22 \\ \times\ 5 \\ \hline \end{array}$

5. $\begin{array}{r} 25 \\ \times\ 9 \\ \hline \end{array}$

6. $\begin{array}{r} 81 \\ \times\ 7 \\ \hline \end{array}$

7. $\begin{array}{r} 11 \\ \times\ 7 \\ \hline \end{array}$

8. $\begin{array}{r} 98 \\ \times\ 4 \\ \hline \end{array}$

9. $\begin{array}{r} 15 \\ \times\ 2 \\ \hline \end{array}$

10. $\begin{array}{r} 93 \\ \times\ 3 \\ \hline \end{array}$

11. $\begin{array}{r} 46 \\ \times\ 5 \\ \hline \end{array}$

12. $\begin{array}{r} 21 \\ \times\ 9 \\ \hline \end{array}$

13. $\begin{array}{r} 87 \\ \times\ 4 \\ \hline \end{array}$

14. $\begin{array}{r} 89 \\ \times\ 5 \\ \hline \end{array}$

15. $\begin{array}{r} 50 \\ \times\ 5 \\ \hline \end{array}$

19. $\begin{array}{r} 33 \\ \times\ 6 \\ \hline \end{array}$

16. $\begin{array}{r} 34 \\ \times\ 7 \\ \hline \end{array}$

20. $\begin{array}{r} 52 \\ \times\ 8 \\ \hline \end{array}$

17. $\begin{array}{r} 69 \\ \times\ 6 \\ \hline \end{array}$

21. $\begin{array}{r} 63 \\ \times\ 4 \\ \hline \end{array}$

18. $\begin{array}{r} 86 \\ \times\ 8 \\ \hline \end{array}$

22. $\begin{array}{r} 20 \\ \times\ 9 \\ \hline \end{array}$

23. $\begin{array}{r} 36 \\ \times\ 9 \\ \hline \end{array}$

24. $\begin{array}{r} 93 \\ \times\ 2 \\ \hline \end{array}$

25. $\begin{array}{r} 11 \\ \times\ 5 \\ \hline \end{array}$

26. $\begin{array}{r} 28 \\ \times\ 5 \\ \hline \end{array}$

27. $\begin{array}{r} 68 \\ \times\ 4 \\ \hline \end{array}$

28. $\begin{array}{r} 14 \\ \times\ 9 \\ \hline \end{array}$

29. $\begin{array}{r} 38 \\ \times\ 7 \\ \hline \end{array}$

30. $\begin{array}{r} 88 \\ \times\ 2 \\ \hline \end{array}$

31. $\begin{array}{r} 48 \\ \times\ 6 \\ \hline \end{array}$

32. $\begin{array}{r} 43 \\ \times\ 6 \\ \hline \end{array}$

33. $\begin{array}{r} 68 \\ \times\ 9 \\ \hline \end{array}$

34. $\begin{array}{r} 70 \\ \times\ 2 \\ \hline \end{array}$

35. $\begin{array}{r} 40 \\ \times\ 6 \\ \hline \end{array}$

36. $\begin{array}{r} 13 \\ \times\ 5 \\ \hline \end{array}$

37. $\begin{array}{r} 68 \\ \times\ 2 \\ \hline \end{array}$

38. $\begin{array}{r} 49 \\ \times\ 6 \\ \hline \end{array}$

39. $\begin{array}{r} 36 \\ \times\ 8 \\ \hline \end{array}$

40. $\begin{array}{r} 32 \\ \times\ 4 \\ \hline \end{array}$

41. $\begin{array}{r} 41 \\ \times\ 8 \\ \hline \end{array}$

42. $\begin{array}{r} 30 \\ \times\ 3 \\ \hline \end{array}$

43. $\begin{array}{r} 13 \\ \times\ 3 \\ \hline \end{array}$

44. $\begin{array}{r} 22 \\ \times\ 7 \\ \hline \end{array}$

45. $\begin{array}{r} 70 \\ \times\ 6 \\ \hline \end{array}$

46. $\begin{array}{r} 71 \\ \times\ 6 \\ \hline \end{array}$

47. $\begin{array}{r} 91 \\ \times\ 4 \\ \hline \end{array}$

48. $\begin{array}{r} 52 \\ \times\ 2 \\ \hline \end{array}$

49. $\begin{array}{r} 98 \\ \times\ 8 \\ \hline \end{array}$

50. $\begin{array}{r} 48 \\ \times\ 6 \\ \hline \end{array}$

51. $\begin{array}{r} 88 \\ \times\ 2 \\ \hline \end{array}$

52. $\begin{array}{r} 44 \\ \times\ 5 \\ \hline \end{array}$

53. $\begin{array}{r} 14 \\ \times\ 3 \\ \hline \end{array}$

54. $\begin{array}{r} 11 \\ \times\ 9 \\ \hline \end{array}$

55. $\begin{array}{r} 82 \\ \times\ 9 \\ \hline \end{array}$

56. $\begin{array}{r} 28 \\ \times\ 9 \\ \hline \end{array}$

57. $\begin{array}{r} 84 \\ \times\ 2 \\ \hline \end{array}$

58. $\begin{array}{r} 30 \\ \times\ 3 \\ \hline \end{array}$

59. $\begin{array}{r} 14 \\ \times\ 7 \\ \hline \end{array}$

60. $\begin{array}{r} 88 \\ \times\ 6 \\ \hline \end{array}$

61. $\begin{array}{r} 17 \\ \times\ 2 \\ \hline \end{array}$

62. $\begin{array}{r} 33 \\ \times\ 8 \\ \hline \end{array}$

63. $\begin{array}{r} 23 \\ \times\ 6 \\ \hline \end{array}$

64. $\begin{array}{r} 68 \\ \times\ 4 \\ \hline \end{array}$

65. $\begin{array}{r} 25 \\ \times\ 2 \\ \hline \end{array}$

66. $\begin{array}{r} 47 \\ \times\ 7 \\ \hline \end{array}$

67. $\begin{array}{r} 29 \\ \times\ 5 \\ \hline \end{array}$

68. $\begin{array}{r} 76 \\ \times\ 9 \\ \hline \end{array}$

69. $\begin{array}{r} 57 \\ \times\ 3 \\ \hline \end{array}$

70. $\begin{array}{r} 41 \\ \times\ 4 \\ \hline \end{array}$

71. $\begin{array}{r} 34 \\ \times\ 4 \\ \hline \end{array}$

72. $\begin{array}{r} 98 \\ \times\ 3 \\ \hline \end{array}$

73. $\begin{array}{r} 65 \\ \times\ 2 \\ \hline \end{array}$

74. $\begin{array}{r} 47 \\ \times\ 5 \\ \hline \end{array}$

75. $\begin{array}{r} 29 \\ \times\ 3 \\ \hline \end{array}$

76. $\begin{array}{r} 76 \\ \times\ 9 \\ \hline \end{array}$

77. $\begin{array}{r} 59 \\ \times\ 7 \\ \hline \end{array}$

78. $\begin{array}{r} 12 \\ \times\ 8 \\ \hline \end{array}$

79. $\begin{array}{r} 21 \\ \times\ 8 \\ \hline \end{array}$

80. $\begin{array}{r} 45 \\ \times\ 7 \\ \hline \end{array}$

81. $\begin{array}{r} 74 \\ \times\ 7 \\ \hline \end{array}$

82. $\begin{array}{r} 36 \\ \times\ 6 \\ \hline \end{array}$

83. $\begin{array}{r} 44 \\ \times\ 8 \\ \hline \end{array}$

84. $\begin{array}{r} 81 \\ \times\ 9 \\ \hline \end{array}$

85. $\begin{array}{r} 87 \\ \times\ 9 \\ \hline \end{array}$

86. $\begin{array}{r} 51 \\ \times\ 3 \\ \hline \end{array}$

87. $\begin{array}{r} 17 \\ \times\ 4 \\ \hline \end{array}$

91. $\begin{array}{r} 45 \\ \times\ 7 \\ \hline \end{array}$

88. $\begin{array}{r} 17 \\ \times\ 3 \\ \hline \end{array}$

92. $\begin{array}{r} 53 \\ \times\ 2 \\ \hline \end{array}$

89. $\begin{array}{r} 92 \\ \times\ 8 \\ \hline \end{array}$

93. $\begin{array}{r} 17 \\ \times\ 7 \\ \hline \end{array}$

90. $\begin{array}{r} 48 \\ \times\ 2 \\ \hline \end{array}$

94. $\begin{array}{r} 50 \\ \times\ 3 \\ \hline \end{array}$

95. $\begin{array}{r} 64 \\ \times\ 5 \\ \hline \end{array}$

96. $\begin{array}{r} 15 \\ \times\ 7 \\ \hline \end{array}$

97. $\begin{array}{r} 57 \\ \times\ 9 \\ \hline \end{array}$

98. $\begin{array}{r} 76 \\ \times\ 9 \\ \hline \end{array}$

99. $\begin{array}{r} 55 \\ \times\ 9 \\ \hline \end{array}$

100. $\begin{array}{r} 19 \\ \times\ 2 \\ \hline \end{array}$

101. $\begin{array}{r} 83 \\ \times\ 5 \\ \hline \end{array}$

102. $\begin{array}{r} 37 \\ \times\ 2 \\ \hline \end{array}$

Mental Division

Solve.

1. 80 ÷ 8 = ______

2. 10 ÷ 5 = ______

3. 18 ÷ 2 = ______

4. 60 ÷ 10 = ______

5. 28 ÷ 7 = ______

6. 8 ÷ 8 = ______

7. 60 ÷ 5 = ______

8. 9 ÷ 9 = ______

9. 80 ÷ 10 = ______

10. 12 ÷ 2 = ______

11. 120 ÷ 12 = ______

12. 18 ÷ 9 = ______

13. 25 ÷ 5 = ______

14. 24 ÷ 8 = ______

15. 77 ÷ 11 = ______

16. 24 ÷ 12 = ______

17. 24 ÷ 2 = ______

18. 6 ÷ 6 = ______

19. 16 ÷ 4 = ______

20. 96 ÷ 8 = ______

21. 132 ÷ 12 = ______

22. 99 ÷ 9 = ______

23. 44 ÷ 4 = ______

24. 110 ÷ 11 = ______

25. 96 ÷ 12 = ______

26. 90 ÷ 10 = ______

27. 21 ÷ 3 = ______

28. 12 ÷ 1 = ______

29. 10 ÷ 10 = ______

30. 36 ÷ 6 = ______

31. 84 ÷ 7 = ______

32. 11 ÷ 11 = ______

33. 54 ÷ 6 = ______

34. 120 ÷ 10 = ______

35. 36 ÷ 12 = ______

36. 50 ÷ 5 = ______

37. 70 ÷ 10 = ______

38. 56 ÷ 8 = ______

39. 90 ÷ 10 = ______

40. 55 ÷ 11 = ______

41. 96 ÷ 12 = ______

42. 84 ÷ 12 = ______

43. 4 ÷ 2 = ______

44. 60 ÷ 12 = ______

45. $12 \div 1 =$ ______

46. $20 \div 5 =$ ______

47. $99 \div 9 =$ ______

48. $9 \div 9 =$ ______

49. $88 \div 11 =$ ______

50. $36 \div 6 =$ ______

51. $77 \div 11 =$ ______

52. $16 \div 2 =$ ______

53. $14 \div 7 =$ ______

54. $24 \div 8 =$ ______

55. $16 \div 4 =$ ______

56. $55 \div 5 =$ ______

57. $30 \div 10 =$ ______

58. $64 \div 8 =$ ______

59. $24 \div 12 =$ ______

60. $42 \div 7 =$ ______

61. $42 \div 7 =$ ______

62. $70 \div 10 =$ ______

63. $24 \div 4 =$ ______

64. $33 \div 11 =$ ______

65. $63 \div 7 =$ ______

66. $27 \div 9 =$ ______

67. $4 \div 1 =$ ______

68. $50 \div 10 =$ ______

69. $12 \div 3 =$ ______

70. $55 \div 5 =$ ______

71. $35 \div 5 =$ ______

72. $35 \div 7 =$ ______

73. $12 \div 6 =$ ______

74. $60 \div 10 =$ ______

75. $120 \div 10 =$ ______

76. $36 \div 4 =$ ______

77. 33 ÷ 3 = ______

78. 96 ÷ 8 = ______

79. 54 ÷ 9 = ______

80. 30 ÷ 6 = ______

81. 56 ÷ 7 = ______

82. 21 ÷ 7 = ______

83. 15 ÷ 3 = ______

84. 110 ÷ 10 = ______

85. 80 ÷ 10 = ______

86. 18 ÷ 9 = ______

87. 50 ÷ 5 = ______

88. 88 ÷ 8 = ______

89. 11 ÷ 11 = ______

90. 14 ÷ 2 = ______

91. 90 ÷ 9 = ______

92. 22 ÷ 11 = ______

93. $2 \div 2 =$ ______

94. $6 \div 1 =$ ______

95. $24 \div 6 =$ ______

96. $120 \div 12 =$ ______

97. $10 \div 1 =$ ______

98. $4 \div 4 =$ ______

99. $21 \div 7 =$ ______

100. $66 \div 6 =$ ______

101. $5 \div 1 =$ ______

102. $96 \div 12 =$ ______

103. $108 \div 9 =$ ______

104. $88 \div 11 =$ ______

105. $16 \div 8 =$ ______

106. $9 \div 3 =$ ______

107. $121 \div 11 =$ ______

108. $48 \div 12 =$ ______

109. 63 ÷ 9 = ______

110. 10 ÷ 5 = ______

111. 70 ÷ 10 = ______

112. 50 ÷ 5 = ______

113. 42 ÷ 6 = ______

114. 28 ÷ 4 = ______

115. 54 ÷ 9 = ______

116. 24 ÷ 4 = ______

117. 18 ÷ 6 = ______

118. 20 ÷ 5 = ______

119. 70 ÷ 7 = ______

120. 44 ÷ 11 = ______

121. 66 ÷ 11 = ______

122. 66 ÷ 6 = ______

123. 66 ÷ 11 = ______

124. 66 ÷ 6 = ______

Long Division

Solve.

1. $5\overline{)745}$

3. $2\overline{)866}$

2. $3\overline{)387}$

4. $3\overline{)225}$

5. $2\overline{)636}$

6. $4\overline{)928}$

7. $2\overline{)180}$

8. $5\overline{)810}$

9. $3\overline{)834}$

10. $4\overline{)932}$

11. $8 \overline{)600}$

12. $6 \overline{)150}$

13. $3 \overline{)186}$

14. $7 \overline{)497}$

15. $6 \overline{)696}$

16. $2 \overline{)498}$

17. $2\overline{)736}$

18. $3\overline{)216}$

19. $5\overline{)845}$

20. $3\overline{)183}$

21. $6\overline{)276}$

22. $3\overline{)285}$

Multiply in Columns

1. 679
2. 44
3. 168
4. 110
5. 225
6. 567
7. 77
8. 392
9. 30
10. 279
11. 230
12. 189
13. 348
14. 445
15. 250
16. 238
17. 414
18. 688
19. 198
20. 416
21. 252
22. 180
23. 324
24. 186
25. 55
26. 140
27. 272
28. 126
29. 266
30. 176
31. 288
32. 258
33. 612
34. 140
35. 240
36. 65
37. 136
38. 294
39. 288
40. 128
41. 328
42. 90
43. 39
44. 154
45. 420
46. 426
47. 364
48. 104

49. 784
50. 288
51. 176
52. 220
53. 42
54. 99
55. 738
56. 252
57. 168
58. 90
59. 98
60. 528
61. 34
62. 264
63. 138
64. 272
65. 50
66. 329
67. 145
68. 684
69. 171
70. 164
71. 136
72. 294
73. 130
74. 235
75. 87
76. 684
77. 413
78. 96
79. 168
80. 315
81. 518
82. 216
83. 352
84. 729
85. 783
86. 153
87. 68
88. 51
89. 736
90. 96
91. 315
92. 106
93. 119
94. 150
95. 320
96. 105
97. 513
98. 684
99. 495
100. 38
101. 415
102. 74

Mental Division

1. 10
2. 2
3. 9
4. 6
5. 4
6. 1
7. 12
8. 1
9. 8
10. 6
11. 10
12. 2
13. 5
14. 3
15. 7
16. 2
17. 12
18. 1
19. 4
20. 12
21. 11
22. 11
23. 11
24. 10
25. 8
26. 9
27. 7
28. 12
29. 1
30. 6
31. 12
32. 1
33. 9
34. 12
35. 3
36. 10
37. 7
38. 7
39. 9
40. 5
41. 8
42. 7
43. 2
44. 5
45. 12
46. 4
47. 11
48. 1
49. 8
50. 6
51. 7
52. 8
53. 2
54. 3
55. 4
56. 11
57. 3
58. 8
59. 2
60. 6
61. 6
62. 7
63. 6
64. 3
65. 9
66. 3
67. 4
68. 5
69. 4
70. 11
71. 7
72. 5
73. 2
74. 6
75. 12
76. 9
77. 11
78. 12
79. 6
80. 5

81.	8	90.	7	99.	3	108.	4	117.	3
82.	3	91.	10	100.	11	109.	7	118.	4
83.	5	92.	2	101.	5	110.	2	119.	10
84.	11	93.	1	102.	8	111.	7	120.	4
85.	8	94.	6	103.	12	112.	10	121.	6
86.	2	95.	4	104.	8	113.	7	122.	11
87.	10	96.	10	105.	2	114.	7	123.	6
88.	11	97.	10	106.	3	115.	6	124.	11
89.	1	98.	1	107.	11	116.	6		

Long Division

1.	149	7.	90	13.	62	19.	169
2.	129	8.	162	14.	71	20.	61
3.	433	9.	278	15.	116	21.	46
4.	75	10.	233	16.	249	22.	95
5.	318	11.	75	17.	368		
6.	232	12.	25	18.	72		

www.ingramcontent.com/pod-product-compliance
Lightning Source LLC
LaVergne TN
LVHW060514170826
845677LV00026B/1757
9798869451507